MW01230409

The
Lost Indian

The
Lost Indian

Jimit Kapadia

TWISTED ROOSTER
PUBLISHING

ISBN-13:
979-8-218-21886-7 Paperback
979-8-218-21887-4 Hardcover

LCCN: 2023910159

Twisted Rooster Publishing
Melbourne, Florida

Table of Content

Acknowledgements

I would love to thank a lot of people who have left a print in my life and who have contributed to the person I am today. I did not want to mention specific names with the fear of leaving someone out, so I decided to share my gratitude as follows.

First, I want to acknowledge my parents who have given me a wonderful life by raising me with proper values, manners, morals, and principles that have become my treasures forever. A special thanks to my mom who still to this day continues to support me and all my adventures, career, and dreams. She has always believed in me and for that, I am very thankful.

Secondly, I want to thank all of my close friends who have given me the strength, support, and have believed in me since day one. They all know who they are without me having to name them. They have always stood by my side. Without them in my life I would not have the confidence in myself that I have today. I really thank them.

I also thank my colleagues and leaders in my professional role who have given me the opportunity to believe that I can achieve all the goals I propose myself. They have cleared the path for me so that I could climb the corporate ladder and enter the white-collar corporate world.

All the customers that come into my bar every week and help keep the doors open for people of all walks of life. They have contributed to the positive impact we have made in the community in Melbourne. Their feedback and even constructive criticism has continuously contributed to our successful trajectory.

To everyone who has supported me
along the way, THANK YOU! #loveus.

The Man Behind The Man

P eople say that when the time is right, you will know it. This is a term applied to many areas in life such as: when to start a relationship, when to go into business, when to take the next step in any given area, and in my case, when to write a book. It might seem like a simple task, but the paper will hold whatever we decide to write, and what we do end up writing will last many years, beyond our time assigned on earth. So, I knew that putting together the pages of my life story was something that had to carry a higher purpose. I didn't want just another story to be told. It had to inspire other people that will feel represented and identified with my life, so that they too can find the inspiration to go after their dreams and not fall short from what they deserve.

Many who have met me and have heard some of my stories, my trials, and the circumstances that I have overcome, have suggested that I write a book sharing my experiences. But in all honesty, it just didn't feel like it was the moment to do it. There were just too many things out of place and needing to be organized, that I couldn't see myself investing time to write when I needed every ounce of energy to make things work around me. Time continued to pass, and pieces of my life started to fall where they needed to be and like a puzzle, everything started to come together. The desire to share my story continued to grow stronger than ever. Because of the many roles that I carry as a son, caretaker, professional, business owner, and entrepreneur, I have always been exposed to different scenarios and life stories of other people. With each of them my desire to tell my own personal story grew stronger and I knew I could not avoid it for long. In fact, I didn't want to put it off anymore. It was the season to shine light and tribute to the many factors and people that have contributed to the person I have become today.

Now, I am finally at a season of my life that I feel it's the right time to share my full story; all of who I am, everything that I have overcome and achieved have made this a true fairy tale in the making. I want to share my story with people that I know, as well as with people that might find inspiration in these pages. When I finally sat down to write this book, I came to the conclusion that up to this point, my editor was the only one that now truly knew the real Jimit Kapadia. I had not spoken or shared to anyone else besides my mother all of the aspects that have made me the person I am today. Not one person really knew my full story. Many thoughts ran through my mind. Will people actually read my story? Will they be inspired with what I share, or will I be judged by it? I was excited yet a bit anxious to see or listen to the first reactions of those that have found out that I finally decided to start this journey. I had been so busy making things happen for everyone around me, my family, the community, friends, and including things that are part of my life today, that I had been putting this project aside, but the time has come. Despite the mental war between my thoughts, I still felt the need to share because there are many "Jimits" out there probably seeking a life purpose and not knowing how their current situations can play into what they will become tomorrow. Our life is a book, each day is a new page and the seasons we live are the chapters. I have gone through many seasons, changes, transformations, wins and losses and I can reaffirm that each one has worked together for the greater good. This includes coming across the people that helped me put together the book that you now have in your hands today. This is not an ordinary story. It is a life testimony of a man that has connected with his essence and with the purpose for which he was placed into this experience called *life*. I have been blessed with the story of so many people and today I want to share with you my own with the hope that you will be able to love yourself, strive for excellence, connect with your spirit, and have the ability to see the colors in a black and white dominated world. Why settle for one crayon to paint with if there are many colors in the box? Dare to be you and #loveus.

NOT AN ORDINARY STORY

As long as I can think back and remember, I have always known that I was born with a higher purpose and that I was not an ordinary man. Nothing in my life from my childhood to adulthood has been ordinary. I have always felt that life was meant to be lived with intention, passion, and joy. Whoever has come in direct contact with me or has followed me on social media can definitely confirm that my personality and the drive behind my actions are loud, colorful, and intentional. I don't leave anything to chance. I was born and raised in the city known to many as the heart of the Bollywood film industry, on the west coast of the country with spectacular waterfronts, and very dense in population, one of India's largest cities, Mumbai.

Mumbai is a very populated urban city that always has something happening. It is never quiet and it's a cultural mix of personalities. A metropolitan beauty with a deep natural harbor. In comparison, it's like combining the busy New York City vibe with the street food vendors, the hustle and bustle of many things happening at the same time, the large crowds, trains, buses, and craziness, combined with the Hollywood, California feel. The only additional things you will see added to all this beautiful chaos are all of the different animals running along-side the streets like horses, cows, goats, and occasionally buf-falos... normal! This was the lifestyle I knew and grew up to love. This is the reason I think that silence is suffocating. Because it is one of the most visited cities in India, I have been blessed to have been exposed to different people, languages, cultures, and religions since I was a young boy. I was able to learn five lan-guages in my childhood. In school I learned the national and state language, at home I learned my mother tongue, my pri-mary in school was English and I took three years of French that unfortunately today, I can barely recall. Besides the traditional *bonjour (hello), au revoir (goodbye), merci (thank you), oui (yes), et comment allez-vous (how are you)* ... the only memory I have left of this language is the French Kiss!

I grew up with an extensive family because in these days, your neighbors became part of your immediate family. My par-ents, although they raised me with traditional Hindu values, they decided to place me in a primary English-speaking School. You might think this act of enrolling me at this school is some-thing normal to do, because the more well-rounded a person can be, the more benefits they will see in their lives; but this was not the typical scenario for Indian parents to do and it was not the case for my parents. This was not necessarily well viewed back then in our community. Many of our relatives, close friends, and even neighbors did not understand why my parents made this decision and they did not agree with it. To this day, this is something that I admire of my parents, especially my mother because she was willing to accept the challenge of going against the 'status quo'. My parents didn't know English, so when they decided this for my life, they didn't have a plan in their minds of how they would help me learn a language they themselves did not know. How were they going to help me with my home-work? They didn't have the resources to pay for tutors or private teachers to help with the language, but these mental arguments did not stop them. My dad was very determined and felt strong about his decision. He firmly believed I was capable of reaching milestones he was not able to achieve. This is a quality I can confess to take after him. He was my model. He taught me that once you see a vision and you want to have this as a goal, you go after it and make it happen. If you want it strong enough, you will always find a way to make it possible. This was my foundation. This was what was taught to me, to have a goal driven mentality.

PUSH AND MAKE IT POSSIBLE

We were not a wealthy family; we were a middle-class Indian family just trying to survive and make ends meet on a daily basis. But despite any limitations, both my parents were very strong willed and had the desire to live a different lifestyle, especially through their children. My dad lost his parents when he was seven years of age and a distant relative's grandmother took him in and raised him and his siblings. He didn't receive any inher-itance, so from a young boy he had to hustle and work hard for the things he desired. Nothing was handed to him. The only things that he was given were a good example in showing good manners, being respectful to others, embracing the culture, and just simply humanity.

As a family we were always working hard and making sure that everyone was well taken care of, and my dad always took it upon himself to put food on the table. He was the first role model I had of what hard work looked like. I saw him go from being a door-to-door salesman, to selling spices and condi-ments, as well as other products to small shops and to street vendors progressing little by little, to then eventually having his own business and becoming a business owner. Back then not everyone in India had color television or VCRS, so he started collecting them and created a rental shop where people could come and rent a VCR and/or a color television for the weekend and for special occasions. He grew and developed a business all on his own. My father always had a great mentality for business, and this has been one of the best gifts that he has given me; the example of striving for excellence and going after what you have always wanted.

My mother on the other hand has always been very sharp and savvy and knew how to run the business from a management perspective. She worked on schedules, deliveries, orders, making sure that everyone had what they requested, and that all customer needs were catered to. All this in addition to being a wife and a fulltime mother, taking care of the house, helping with homework, and just with everything in general. To this day I am still in awe of all that she has done and what she is capable of still achieving. She always wanted to be a lawyer and I am fully convinced that if she had gone after this dream, she would have been one of the best. At the time of this book, she is 86 years old, and I believe she could still be a CSI Agent with her sharpness. Nothing can get past her still today.

MY OWN WONDER WOMAN

I have very fond memories of my mother when I think back to my childhood years and the example that she set for me. I have a specific memory tattooed in my mind of her strength and courage. I can recall that it had been a rainy season in Mumbai and the streets were flooded. I had never seen a flood before, and I was very scared. In the middle of all of this chaos I still had to go to school because classes were not suspended. Mom wanted to make sure that I was able to get on the school bus safely, so she carried me on her hips all the way to the bus so that I would not be dragged by the waters. While she was trying to get me safely to the other side, she lost the house key and had no way of getting back in. She had to contact and wait for a locksmith to come and help while being drenched, cold and wet. It was a whole ordeal, but she made sure that I was ok. She risked her life just to get me to school safely because she truly believed I was born for greatness. I never found out about this incident until as an adult already, my father mentioned how committed she was to help me reach my highest potential.

My main education was in a British-Catholic School with English as my primary language. My education experience since kindergarten had been exposing me to different languages and cultures, so my mind was absorbing everything around me. The best education my parents gave me did not come from any books but from within their life's testimonies. This was not just in business, but in all aspects of life. Still, they enrolled me in a Catholic School just so that I would have the best education available at the time and learn to be well rounded. There, every Monday in the assembly we would gather to sing *"Thy Father in heaven, Holy be thy name,"* we celebrated Christmas and Easter, and then I would celebrate the *Diwali* – our holy festival. Thanks to them, I was always surrounded by different types of cultural and spiritual beliefs. Because there is such a variety of beliefs in Mumbai from Catholics, Christians, Hindu's, to Muslims, it was almost an extension of what I experienced within the city. There was always something being celebrated. My parents made sure that I learned everything about our gods from *lord ganesha* also called *Ganpati*, elephant-headed Hindu god of beginnings, who is traditionally worshipped before any major enterprise; to the *goddess mataji* and how they protect. They wanted me to always remember my roots and where I come from. My parents taught me mythology and the stories of our gods. I also learned the story of Jesus Christ in school and how you could be saved; I learned about reincarnation and stories of hell and purgatory. I have learned it all. The beauty of it is that there is a beautiful and mysterious connection between all of them.

I love this about my culture. There was no way possible that you were not exposed one way or another to the human diversity that is accessible in India. I also grew up with the traditional expectations of an Indian son who has the responsibility of carrying on the family name, legacy, and all of the responsibilities it entailed. I was responsible for providing the family food, shelter, and water. All of them! Back then, the majority of men were the bread winners and sole providers for the home. Women were expected to be the home caretakers and raise the children under the traditional customs. This has now evolved and many women today in India, like in America, are able to provide for their families, but growing up, I had this expectation on my shoulders that one day I would have to be the sole provider for my parents. I will admit that there were many moments that the thoughts of this responsibility was overwhelming. I was full of certain uncertainties but somehow, I knew that it would all be all right. And I can say that it has been. I took care of my father until his last day on earth and I am proud to have honored him until his very last day.

Speaking about this time of my life has just made me reflect more on the emotional effects our environment inflicts on us. If I could travel back in time and stand in front of myself at that age, I would tell him: "listen to your heart but take your mind with you. Make sure you make a plan and stick to it if your heart tells you to. Always pray and keep in mind that life will be tough, it will take you through rocky roads, but make sure to enjoy the fruit of the journey. Never give up on your dreams." And in the same way I am sure that my future self is saying, *"Why didn't I start this sooner?"* Everything I was being exposed to would become a puzzle piece I would later see how it fits perfectly into the person I was becoming. I was not able to see the overall image yet, but every life experience was a necessary puzzle piece in the beautiful experience called life.

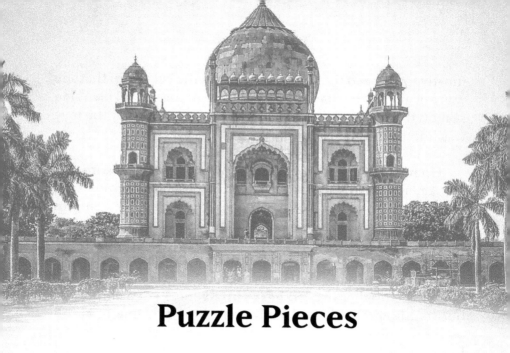

Puzzle Pieces

I am a firm believer that who we are meant to be will start to manifest very early in our lives beginning in our childhood years. For example, people with artistic abilities testify that they always remember themselves playing music or singing and dancing since they were very little. They visit their childhood memories, and they can recall how they were always doing what they are passionate about and even have old home videos or pictures that testify to this. Well, I can also say that my first conscious memory that spoke to my purpose and who I was meant to be was when I was about five years old. My mother used to wear the traditional Indian outfits called *Saris*, and I remember I would hold on to the *Saris* and follow her everywhere. I was mesmerized by the colors and the textures of her clothing and how beautiful she looked. The most amazing thing was that she would let me! She carried me around and allowed me to be part of her life as much as possible since she was the one who spent the most time with me. She was the person who mostly took me to the school bus and on the occasions that she was not able to, my dad used to take me to the school on a side seat on the bicycle. We were not a wealthy family, but the love was unmeasurable.

On my first day of kindergarten my mother made sure that I looked my best. She dressed me with gray shorts, white short sleeve shirt, and a little tie mind you; I remember going in and feeling scared. I looked around me and I didn't want to be there because I didn't know any of the children and none of the teachers were my mom. When my mother saw my reaction, she stood outside making sure I was ok and stayed there for a while in case the teacher needed her to intervene. I got a glimpse of her standing outside and I did everything possible to climb out of the window and run to her arms. From that moment on, I understood that my mother was my safe place. I knew that no matter what, she would always be the place I would run to when I felt unsafe. She made sure to be present one way or another through all my school years. With her help and inspiration, I was able to finish all the way to tenth grade because in the British School system, tenth grade was the last year. Once completed, I took my board exam and anxiously waited for the results to know what college I could pick. This would then represent my junior and senior year in a Junior college and move on to the final three years for my bachelor's degree. Through it all from beginning to end, my mother was very present and made sure I felt safe, loved, and secure.

The Beauty Behind the Magic

In between those very important years, I was presented to a whole world full of colors, movements, sounds, lights, and applauses. When I was in first grade, I was exposed to my first stage performance. Although I was only five years old, being in the school chorus and performing on stage captivated me. I fell in love with entertainment. Fast Forward to when I was in fourth grade, I was already playing different roles and scenes in the school dramas. I fell in love with the dramatics, the lights, and the possibility of being someone else while still being in my own skin. Because it was an only boys school, they needed someone to play the female roles in the dramas, and yes... I dressed up at that age and always received a standing ovation. Now, let me clarify that my participation in these pieces did not weigh in who I am today. At that age you do not understand what attraction is and even less, what an attraction of human-to-human nature may be. I was just in love with everything the world of arts had to offer. I fell head over heels for the fabrics and textures, the patterns, and all of the makeup. It was mesmerizing! I loved what I did, and the school took notice. I always had lead roles all the way up to the eighth grade.

There was a pivotal moment that I experience that exposed me to yet another side of entertainment I did not know I would dominate. I became very chatty in the classroom one day when the teacher was absent, and after being exposed by the class monitor to the principal, I was reported to the principal's office. His punishment was to take away my participation from the main drama piece of the school during the parent's day show. I was devastated. I didn't understand why someone would see banding a person from performing their talents as a good punishment. Little did I know was that all of the teachers tried to convince him of letting me return to the stage. They were convinced the show wouldn't be the same without me. When they were not able to make him budge from his decision, they decided to give me another role and found a way for me to participate despite of his desires. They made me a choreographer for the show! So, in my eighth-grade year, I choreographed the Parent Day Competition Show for the fifth graders and helped them connect to their talents. Needless to say, they won first place and even the principal ended up acknowledging that no matter where they placed me, my talents and passion for the arts would always have a huge impact on others. I continued to perform in dramas and plays all the way up to my college years where the plays were now more complex, and it gave me the opportunity to see what a more professional scenario was like. Take note and be aware that your purpose will follow you; your essence will shine through any circumstance or situation. I was blessed to have teachers in my life that saw something special in me and made a way for me to shine. There will always be people that are able to see much more in you than maybe you see in yourself, the secret is to make sure that the people you allow to have a voice in your life are those that add value and build you up. What we are meant to be, we will be; and there is no stopping that.

Proud Momma's Boy

I can proudly and honestly say I am 100 percent a momma's boy! I can feel her heart strings and I know that she can feel mine. Then and now, my mom has always made me feel loved. She is without a doubt the strongest voice I have had in my life. You would probably not believe me today based on who I have become, but back then, in my early days I used to be one of the shiest and timid boys there could be. I was constantly afraid and had no confidence in myself whatsoever. Yes, the same boy that shined on stage, off the stage I felt lost. I did not know who I would be if I didn't have my mother there telling me what to do. A lot of the security and self-awareness that I proudly manifest today is in large part due to my mother's love and acceptance. She changed me and changed the way I see the world. Having been so close to her heart also helped me to understand a woman's point of view and it gave me a healthy perspective to be in touch with my emotions. I saw the real struggles that many women like her faced. Not only their struggles but the way they each had to be an anchor, the force within the family and how many of them felt they had to always be strong. I inherited from her the generosity, caring, honesty, integrity, to love and to be proud. Little by little her example was forming an extraordinary version of me. People who see me today that knew me from India, are completely astonished as to who I have become. They cannot believe my personal transformation.

My mother has never stopped evolving, so I have to make sure to keep up with her! She is the eldest of her siblings today and she was the first to learn how to work with an *iPad*, *iPhone*, and do video calls and messaging. She makes the effort to communicate in English with her caregivers and she is constantly asking about the new technology that comes out. She always wants to learn. She taught me that the day you stop learning, is the day you stop growing. She is a rock star. If she never stopped evolving, how can I?

She has given me the best life examples continuously and she taught me how to truly love without exceptions. One of the passions that I love sharing with her are the cruises and what I enjoy during those vacations. I love doing cruises and meeting people from all over the world, watching the shows and listening to the music. I enjoy all the arts available. I have done many from local to international as well as gay cruises. Those are a hoot! I feel the same freedom there as when I stepped for the first time in the United States. After dad passed, I made sure that she enjoyed life to the fullest. I remember on one occasion I took her on an Alaska cruise trip. I will never forget seeing this little one, dressed in one of my drench coats and when the ship was approaching this huge iceberg, even though we had a balcony, I decided to take her to the pool deck. It was breathtaking. If you don't believe in God or the opportunity to see heaven on earth, take a cruise to Alaska. You will definitely be convinced. There I was standing in front of a huge masterpiece from mother nature, in amazement and in awe, and I was taking it all in while holding my mother's hand in the process. It seemed as though this beautiful glacier was headed straight towards us, and it felt like a blessing from God showering over us. All I could do was let the tears fall. They were not tears of joy or sorrow, but rather the human feeling of that moment in which my hands were holding hers. It was a full circle moment. I still had my mom by my side despite all of her health issues and the things that she has had to overcome including major heart surgery. My mother is the bravest person I know. She has never stopped amazing me since I was a little boy until this very day.

She always made sure to educate me in all of our traditional rituals. She was the one who made me believe in God and made me worship. She never limited me to one style, one religion or one vision. She wanted me to be very well versed about everything. This is why you need to make sure that the mirrors you decide to look in are mirrors that can point you in the right direction and push you to be the best version of yourself that you can be. Today, I take full care of her because it's the life cycle. I love pampering her, seeing her smile, because I have witnessed everything she has ever gone through since I was a baby. So, because of all of her efforts in life, I have decided to make her my priority until the day of her passing. She is my strength and my weakness. She always brings out the best of me.

First Love

There are different kinds of love with layers, textures, and dimensions. My mother's love has been the most intense and pure love I have felt. Without a doubt it was the one that taught me to love myself. But I can recall feeling *in love* for the first time with another person like me when I was sixteen and in tenth grade. He was a very special person and even though we were both young, in school, fully aware of our emotions and feelings, in the back of our minds we knew that this would not be a fruitful relationship. It would never develop to be a traditional relationship as we see them today. Nevertheless, it was a special season that I carry in my heart because although the world around me wasn't aware of who I was becoming, life has always allowed for special people to truly see me. It's complicated to find the correct ways to express in words what this relationship meant, but it was my first exposure to what finding a soulmate would be. I would wake up in the morning when the phone rang, and it was him calling. Twenty other people could have called the house and my sleep was never interrupted, but when he decided to phone the house, automatically my soul would stir inside me, and I immediately would open my eyes. It was that crazy!

Finally, when we started prepping for our college days, we started to drift apart, and things just didn't work out like we wished they had. I was afraid of many things, uncertain about others (moving to America included), so we decided it was best to part ways. I was completely shattered. This was my first broken version, and it was very hard. It took me about four years to get over this heartbreak thinking of what could have been or what could I have done differently, but I do not regret any part of it. Afterall, how many people can say that they felt seen and accepted by another person and felt as if they were your soulmate? It hurt drifting apart, but I am forever grateful that I got to experience that at such a young age.

I promised myself that when I finally set foot in America, in some odd way, I would receive the freedom to truly be myself in every way and form. I could finally be the real me without having to hide or pretend. I could allow myself the opportunity not to be ashamed of my actions and be able to make my own decisions knowing that it was totally on me. While I lived in India, I was still under the traditional expectations of being married under traditional values. Arranged marriages were still very normal. It was rare to see couples marry out of love, in fact it was frowned upon. Marriages were arranged because it was the union of two families and not just the union of two people.

It was a matter of joint families and the benefits it brought to both sides. It was important for both families to feel everything was compatible in all areas. Now, thankfully it evolved into respecting the couple's wishes, but growing up, my parents had this expectation for me as well. Nevertheless, crossing to America also meant taking off the pressure since I arrived at precisely the age, they would traditionally be trying to marry me off. I can still remember coming back to India with my mom for summer vacations and since she was not aware of my sexual preferences, she would try to set me up with different girls to see if something would evolve into a marriage.

As my parents and I learned and integrated to the way of living in the United States and having the freedom to decide, I became very self-motivated and gained an additional drive to take advantage of this new opportunity. My parents did what they had to do in order for me to have this chance; now it was up to me to make the most of it. After I was settled in at Melbourne, Florida, I decided to visit a gay bar for the first time ever, including my time in Mumbai. I decided to honor who I was openly. I made my first ever American gay friend at this bar. To this day we are still very good friends. Taking that step was a milestone and it just made me fall in love even more with this country.

Value What Matters Most

My dad passed away without knowing I was gay. I just never got around to having the official conversation with him. In all truth I just didn't feel I found the right moment to do so. I can't assure you that maybe in his heart he didn't know, it could be that as a dad he already did, but he never pressured me to confess to it or treated me any differently because of it. It wasn't until recently in 2022 that I finally came out to my mother, the most important person in the world. Her opinion was the only one that truly mattered and since she is so advanced in age, I wanted her to know directly from my lips, although moms always know. When I built up the courage, her words to this day still bring me to tears: *"Jimit, do not let anyone tell you that you are in the wrong and don't let anyone say you are not proper."* She has always told me that all she ever wanted in life is to see me happy, and as long as I am, that is all a mother can ask for. Still at 86 years old she was looking for ways to protect and shield my heart. She was speaking purpose into my life. I wasn't ashamed to tell her, I just did not want to add any additional worries to my mother. I knew that if I had told her before, she would constantly be worried for me and wondering if the friends I brought over to the house were "the one" and if so, how would this person make her son happy. It was just additional stress that she did not need, and I just had one goal in mind: make mom happy.

Love has been very hard for me. It is the main area in my life where I have had a rollercoaster of scenarios, but I have yet to live the happily ever after. It's not that I have not tried or even exposed myself to the opportunity, but the results have not been in my favor. I can say however that I have been able to love intensely, and I have also had my heart broken several times. This has managed to make it difficult to trust someone else with it. It is just difficult for me to trust someone else with my heart. I believe this is the reason I have hidden behind my career and entrepreneurship so that I have the perfect distraction. I am learning how to manage and grow in my emotional intelligence because once I come across the correct person, I will be able to grow old next to them. I have not given up, I am just in a still period of my life. When the right person comes along, everything will feel right and there will be no fear. I enjoy seeing how others come together. Being someone's first love is beautiful but being someone's last love will be great. So, in the meantime I am in no hurry to find that special person. I know that their eyes will play a big role because I have always believed that the eyes are the windows to the soul, and you can learn a lot about a person through their eyes. Personality will probably be the second biggest factor because as you might have captured, I am a very loud, vivid, fun-loving, charismatic person and who-ever decides to share their life with me will have the perfect personality to combine with mine. I want to feel proud when bringing them around my business events, or my plus one at different occasions. I want to be sure that they can hold their own and who can appreciate all of us. Life has been really good to me, so I have left it up to destiny to be the one to bring to me that special person and maybe they will bring back to life all of the emotions I have set aside for that special someone.

Life is all about the Drama

Having an acting background has helped me to be able to put on a happy face even when I am crying inside, to act normal even when in all truth my world has been shattered, and to be able to give speeches to hundreds and hundreds of people without hesitation. I have no problem getting on a stage in front of thousands of people without a plan to speak because this was the security that acting gave me. It polished me to the point of increasing the confidence within me. It seems so contradictory that such a powerful tool that I have used throughout my life, has also become the armor I hide behind when I don't want to face my emotions. Sometimes it is easier to play a character and hide behind a different story rather than be my real self.

Having the correct people in my life has been key when I have had to have my breaking moments. I try as much as I can to keep my emotions and my situations to myself, but I am human and there comes a point when we all need someone to lean on. I have been blessed to have an extraordinary circle of friends that allow me to have my moments without any judgements and just making themselves present in my life. There have been countless times that I have broken down and I have just sat

Puzzle Pieces

there in my bar, Bollywood music in the background, drinks at hand and I have just wept. Each time I have done so, there is always someone there to help me pick up the pieces. This is the tribe that allows me to be me, even the broken version. Who would have thought that the results of my entrepreneurship in America would be the place where I would find refuge! Coming to America was the best decision we made, and the fruits will testify to that.

Coming to America

W hen my parents made the decision to move to America, many friends and family members were concerned for my well-being. They were fully aware that things in the United States would be different. People had to do things on their own, and they felt I was not ready for such a drastic change. They knew that I was extremely shy, very codependent, and also told my parents, "He could not do things on his own, he could be easily fooled and has no experience of the real world." They were convinced my parents were making a huge mistake and believed I would become more of a liability to them than an asset. They were worried my parents were willing to invest the little money they had moving to the United States just to give me an opportunity for a better life, but that they would not see a positive outcome. It was a lot for my parents to carry on their shoulders.

But these concerns did not stop my parents from actually taking a chance and following what in their hearts they believed was the best decision for the family. When they finally came over, we had nothing in our pockets, but our hearts were overflowing with hope and determination. See this decision wasn't made lightly. Since I was in school my parents came to the conclusion that they wanted something more for me, so they had started to look into this move for many years. My father applied to get a green card and become a naturalized citizen in 1982 and we received the first interview call ten years later in 1992. They were convinced that coming to America, the land of opportunities, would be the best decision for my future. This is why when I see myself here in the states achieving things, and celebrating milestones I thought would never be possible, I do it for them, because this is what they had made possible for me.

The process in itself was very intense. The interviews were very extensive as well. It felt as if we had committed a crime and we were placed in separate rooms while being interrogated. We had to truly prepare for this. It was not easy. The first interviews were early in the morning, so this included standing outside in a long line in front of the American Embassy in India. I was able to be in the room with my parents because I had signed up to be their translator during the process, so when they were interviewed in English I was there. Amongst the questions they asked, they needed to confirm if we were truly related and who our sponsor would be in America because without one, the green card would not be issued. Our category of classification was by a blood relative, because my dad's younger brother was married to my mom's younger sister. They had been living in Chicago for many years. They went through our finances to make sure that we could afford living in the United States. We went through half a day of medical labs just to prove we had a good bill of health. Once the initial process was approved, my parents received a green card (which by the way is not actually green), and a whole new process began. We received all of the benefits that the American people had except the right to vote. We had to learn everything from scratch.

I crossed over to America when I was twenty years old, but my parents had been speaking about it since I was ten. I was anxiously waiting for the moment to arrive. I would finally see the other side of the world that would open new doors and provide new opportunities for my life. This was good and at the same time it had its downfalls because knowing that this could come at any moment without prior notice, it kept me from doing many things in India. I was afraid of starting new projects since the news could come at any moment. I remember that when my cousins who already lived in America would come back home to India for vacations, I would drown them with questions about the United States. I wanted to know everything I could before crossing over. So, at the age of twenty I got on an airplane for the first time in my life.

When I arrived, I felt lost. Everything was different from what I had envisioned in my mind. I had a different set of references from the American things I liked. My favorite comic book was *Archie*, and I loved the *Tom & Jerry cartoons, Charlie Chaplin* and *Laurel Hardy* as well as *I love Lucy*, so these were my mental references of America. We didn't have a specific plan when we arrived of what we would do or how, we just knew that we crossed over for a higher purpose and now it was up to me to push my parents towards the right direction. The currency was different, so when we paid, we were not sure of how much to give or know if the change we were given was the correct amount. In India, because we were under the British influence, the currency had different values and sizes, here in the United States it's all the same, so I didn't know that the one, five, ten, twenty,fifty and one-hundred-dollar bills were all the same in size. This meant we had to pay close attention when paying that we were handing back the correct bill. We started to learn about the food, the way of living, the full English language as well as the slang which in itself is very hard to learn, basic things like being able to buy a money order in a bank and a post office, the transportation methods, and the general lifestyles.

Growing up in India I honestly thought the rest of the world was the same way and that only a few things changed that made it better. Little did I know that I would end up having to learn everything new from scratch. I remember a funny anecdote now that wasn't as funny back then. I was at the mall filling out job applications and I got hungry. I knew that I wanted to have a burger. So, my first cheeseburger was a Jack in the Box. I stood back for five minutes and observed how three people ordered so that I wouldn't feel so lost. I walked up to the counter, and I ordered my burger. They asked me if I wanted cheese and when I said yes, they said, *"Oh, ok so you want a cheeseburger."* I told the employee I also wanted fries and a soft drink, and the cashier replied, *"Perfect so you want to order a combo meal"*, and I was like, *"No! I just want these three things!"* To me a meal was dinner and all I wanted was a quick bite to eat. To make matters worse, when I ordered the drink, they gave me an empty cup. I started to protest, and they explained that I had to dispense it and serve myself. There I was, once again standing back and observing how others served themselves ice and a soft drink so that I could do the same. The look on their faces was priceless, and even though today I think back, and I can laugh, at the time even those basic daily tasks like ordering a combo were very challenging. It was a lot to take in and because there is so much diversity in the states, we needed to stay focused to learn as much as possible, as quickly as we were able to so that we would stop feeling like tourists and more like residents. This meant that we needed to decide where we would settle down and establish roots because the faster, we did, the sooner I would be able to assume the role of the breadwinner and help my parents. The role was now reversed. I was responsible of their care, their food and shelter. They had done it for me throughout my life, now here in America it was my turn to honor and care for them. It was like I had just become father of two. It never felt as a burden and I never complained. Quite the opposite I was ready for the challenge and I knew that once we settled in the right place, I would not let them down.

Coming to America

After living sometime in the state of Chicago, we made the decision to move to California. We had already been here for over a year and the struggle was 100 percent real. Our family received us and helped a lot, but we were feeling the pressure to do it on our own. Once we were settled in, it was my responsibility to go out looking for a job. So, I would wake up very early in the morning and catch a bus. At 8:00 am I would be sitting on a bus on my way to visit every mall and go to every store filling out job applications, to then catch another bus back home where I would arrive at about 5:00 pm, to do it all again the very next day. It was a challenge. I still remember the three-story malls and having to go to each store with the hope that on any given occasion I would finally receive the call that I had been accepted. After some time passed and I continued seeking a job, I heard someone mention the opportunities available through the job fairs. So, I attended. I ended up at the desk of a Macy's store recruiter and we instantly clicked. It ended up being my first job in America. Now getting there was another ordeal, I had to walk twenty minutes to the first bus stop so that I could take the bus to a train station, from there I would take a train ride to another stop where I crossed the bridge just to take a second train and take the final bus that would take me to the mall where I worked. I had to leave the house three hours before my shift started to ensure I would make it on time. Each way, three hours and four connections. My shifts were nine hours with one hour for lunch, which thankfully I always brought from home because my mother would pack my lunch every day. These lunches were almost always the leftovers from the day before because we were struggling to make things work. So, the shifts started at 12:00 and ended at 9:00 pm every day. This was the life of an immigrant who was chasing the American dream.

After the first five years passed, we needed to wait in order to continue to the next stage. In the process we had to make sure that we were not convicted of any felonies, and this included not being able to leave the country for six months in a row.

Once the five years passed and all was according to the law, we were able to apply for naturalization to see if we qualified. Fortunately, we did!

FACE TO FACE WITH DESTINY

I already shared how I was able to get my first job in Macy's, in the kid's department to help my parents with the cost of living and I had to do the same for my education. I made at the time six dollars and twenty cents an hour ($6.20). But when I was in college, to help with the cost for school I became a professional actor in non-musical broadways. I did weekend shows, one on Fridays, two on Saturdays and one on Sundays; four shows a week! That was my pocket money because I needed to do whatever was necessary in order to finish my education. I am not going to lie, it was very tough at the beginning. Trying to work, study, pursue my dreams and at the same time take care of my parents. California was amazing but the cost of living was hard to keep up with. It was not working for me. Fortunately, my mother's younger sister suggested we move down to Florida. The weather was similar to Mumbai and the cost of living was more affordable than in California. After careful consideration we decided to try it out. We had nothing to lose, and we decided to pack up and move to Melbourne, Florida.

I still remember the first time we came to Melbourne, I was in tears. After living in California, the comparison was very drastic. I thought to myself, *"OMG, I am living in cornfields, wires for traffic lights and dirt roads."* I had always been a city boy and I thought I had made a mistake. But my family insisted we give it a try and my aunt immediately suggest I interview with a local credit union. I started to hunt for the best opportunity I could find. While I did, I remembered when I was a little boy, and I accompanied my father to the bank. I loved it and I always said I wanted to work at a bank when I grew up. Fast forward to this moment when I was seeking an opportunity in the same field of work I admired. This was a full circle.

The day I walked in the main office branch of the credit union, they had three positions available, one full time and two part-time spots. There were other very qualified people out for the same positions, but somehow, I had fallen into grace with the branch manager. There were other candidates with completed bachelor's degrees, but I was the one chosen for the full time slot and the rest were given the part-time positions. I was in awe and humbled by this new role I had been given. I knew that the way we present and carry ourselves is how we are able to build an immediate trust with other people and this will always open doors. For me, I was hired on the spot, and this gave me a huge sense of relief because even though I knew I had a lot to continue learning, I was finally on my way to give my parents the support and lifestyle I had always wanted. I was grateful for my time I had worked at Macy's because this had helped with being able to overcome the currency challenge. Working at the union was giving me the information I needed to continue learning about the checks. The local and out of state checks, traveler's and manager's checks, the policies, procedures, and regulations, it was amazing. It was beyond my imagination. Now, comparing these times in 1993 and currently working at a Fintech company selling software, I am amazed at how it has evolved and how easier it is now versus the times when I began. It's amazing what technology has brought to us. I enjoyed a lot learning everything I could at the credit union. I remained at this position for six months. Then I moved on to a drive-thru teller position which was only for people that could be quick and trustworthy. It was great. We had friendly competitions with the regular tells of who could make the most transactions during a shift. My work was fun! I also loved meeting so many people.

From these positions, I moved on through the call center and customer service positions. I learned about research and disputes, outages and so much more. As I kept learning in every area of the bank, my interest of doing more kept growing. I continued growing within the credit union and I gradually evolved into a loan officer position and underwriter. I ended up managing an e-branch including a team of eighteen women. This was very interesting. Seeing my growth and how far along I had come from arriving and not understanding the worth of the dollar bill I had in my hands, to now having a key role in the banking industry, gave me the confidence to feel that I had made the right decisions. Moving down to Melbourne had been the right move. I had found my true professional calling.

Despite of all the progress I had achieved, I was still making only $24,000-$25,000 a year. That was still not enough for all the things I needed to achieve, so I decided to look for an extra job. I worked full time, Monday to Friday, classic 8-5 at the Credit Union and then from 6:00pm to 9:00pm on Mondays, Wednesdays, and Fridays, and eight hour shifts on the weekends, I used to work at a retail furniture store, managing their paperwork, loan processing for financing their furniture pieces, and other office duties. I only had Tuesdays and Thursdays open, but I took those days to finish the studies I wanted to complete. So, I also went back to college on those two weekdays. That brought in an additional $6-$8 grand a year. It sounds like a lot, and it definitely was, but I had a clear goal in mind, and it was to give my parents the quality of life they deserved.

After five years a friend had applied at a fintech company that the credit union used the software from, and he had told me there was an opening at the Customer Service department and that I should look into it. Sure enough, I went and applied and got the job offer. I remember that I asked the Hiring Manager what the salary for the position was and she asked what my expectations were. Since I do not let any opportunity pass me by, I told her at the time I had two jobs and that I was looking for one full time position that could provide the combination of these two salaries. They started me at $35k which was $3k over what I was currently making. The job came with some challenges, but the reward was worth it. I had to drive 45 minutes each way and I wouldn't be as close to my parents as I wanted. I continued to grow exponentially and within the next five years moved up once again, but now to the sales side of the fintech in this market in which I still work full-time in, and the fruits of my labor have been visible. I never studied finance officially but starting in the banking industry from the bottom up helped me achieve all the milestones and success that I have seen. There even came a time that people would hire me at $1,800 dollars a day just to help them find the "out of balance" issues they had. Looking back at everything, I went from earning $6.20 an hour to earning a six-figure salary. It was a crazy journey towards where I am today. Despite of this, I knew I was doing all of this for them.

Now I overlook a full sales support team and a sales engineers team as well. My acting abilities have been key when presenting to customers and for training my team. It has been a blessing to see them grow and be the best presenters they can be. The department has grown from six people to twenty people today. As an immigrant in this beautiful country, I applaud myself how much I have been able to grow without not having any previous experience. All I had was a "why" and a lot of determination. My "why" were my parents. Growing up with parents who showed me that to have what we want in life, it is all achievable with hard work, was the foundation on which I have built all of my success on.

IT WAS ALL WORTH IT!

My dad passed away in 2002, exactly ten years after we moved to America. He had developed an obstruction jaundice because his gallbladder was full of stones, and it was causing him non-stop hiccups. He was scheduled for surgery, and it was supposed to be an easy procedure. About thirty minutes or so to remove the gallbladder. We were a bit anxious because he was at an early stage of Alzheimer's. The thirty-minute surgery ended up being a four-hour procedure. Suddenly the doctors came out to tell us that things got complicated during the surgery between punctures and bleeding and many medical terms that I still don't know what they are. He ended up in the Intensive Care Unit (ICU). It was heartbreaking for all of us.

I saw my dad continue to deteriorate. I wish I had the power to make this all go away, but all I could do at this time was make sure to be there for him, make myself present and care for him as he had done for me all of my life. I would go by the hospital every day before going to the office because he would only eat from my hand. So, I would feed him and make sure he was fine every single day before starting my own tasks. On December twenty-sixth, the day after Christmas, when I arrived at the office, I heard a page from the receptionist calling my name. She told me that there was an urgent call for me, and they didn't find me at the desk, so they decided to page me. When I finally received the call, I heard the voice of a nurse from the hospital. The only thing that she said to me was, *"I am just calling to tell you that your dad went into cardiac arrest. Please drive safely!"* And she hung up. Nothing else, no additional information or space for me to ask any questions or clear any doubts. Now, not knowing what that meant I was standing there shaken by the news she had just delivered with no clarity. I didn't even know what *cardiac arrest* meant. It was the first time I had heard this medical term. I didn't know what was going on or what to expect. I had a forty-five-minute drive to the hospital, so I started making calls because my biggest concern now was for my mother not to arrive there before I did. I called a friend who only lives fifteen minutes away and I told him, *"Please whatever happens next, and whatever you do, make sure that my mom does not go in before I do."* But being the woman that she is, it was no surprise that when I finally made it to the hospital, my two friends were there waiting for me, and mom had already gone in without me. She had passed out because of the impression the news caused her. She was taken downstairs to the emergency room to be taken care of and I was just trying to compose myself from the blow that had just hit me. I walked in and saw the resuscitation tubes and nurses everywhere and I was even more confused. To add even more stress, I had not yet seen my mother and had no news of her well-being. It took me a minute to realize that my dad had passed, and my mother was in the emergency room, and I had no idea if I would lose them both on that very same day. Not even twenty minutes went by when a nurse came to me to ask what decision I was going to make in regards to my father's body. I just looked at her in disbelief not understanding how she was so cold and unsympathetic at such a delicate moment. I know that doctors and hospital personnel see loss as part of the job, but I was standing in the middle of the hallway having just lost my dad and waiting anxiously to see what was going to happen with my mom. The anger and frustration got the best of me, and I ended up insulting her. I suggested she rethink if she was fit to be an intensive care unit nurse because in my eyes, she didn't fit the role. That was not a "body", that was my dad! It wasn't my intention to be so rude, but I was so hurt and confused, all I wanted to do was be there for my mom. She was the only one I had left.

It was one of the scariest and most painful moments of my life. So many feelings, so many thoughts! All I could do now is pray and believe that everything was going to be all right. I wanted to call my dad's sister who was living in Hong Kong at the time to give her the news, but she was already on a flight on her way to us because we had already told her dad was critical. She had no idea that while she was in the air, dad was passing. Meanwhile, my mother was released from the hospital with no other injuries, other than her heart broken from the loss, and I was relieved to still have her. Now all we needed to do was tell his sister once she arrived, as well as to the rest of the family and start making all the funeral arrangements.

I was in disbelief how in the laps of fourteen days everything changed. We had brought him in to the hospital on the twelfth of December when his symptoms began and on December twenty-six, the day after Christmas my dad passed away. One thing I was proud to cherish was that before dad passed, he was able to see me fulfill one of the goals that as a son I had promised him, and I felt was my responsibility; I had our house built when I was twenty-four years old; four years after coming here. I had promised to take care of them and do my part and before he passed away, and this was one of the milestones he was able to witness and enjoy. I still live in the same house, and I will never leave even if I can afford something bigger, better, or in a different place. This house became a home with both of them in it. It still carries memories of all of us together in every room and it reminds me of my roots and what I was brought over to achieve here in the United States.

When we initially arrived, we lived in a one-bedroom apartment because it was all that we could afford. Keep in mind that my parents didn't know English, so I was taking care of them. I was the sole breadmaker. I worked three jobs and went to college at the same time. After observing the market for a while, I decided to purchase our first and forever home. It was a beautiful and cozy three-bedroom house which my father enjoyed for his last six years on earth. I loved watching my dad enjoy the last six years of his life in our home. I was also able to buy him a car. He was able to proudly drive himself to events, temples, and run every day errands. That was the very first car they had ever owned. He knew his job was done because we would be ok, and I would make sure of that.

Another Strong Blow

During his passing I had to be strong because it was up to me to get everything done and make the arrangements for his funeral, but there was one moment during this process that I was just simply not ready for. In our culture when we die, we get cremated, and I had realized that I was the one who had to push the ignition button for the process to be completed. This included carrying my father in my arms and placing him inside myself. That is how we do it culturally for religious reasons. This is the role of the son. While I was picking up my father's body I could only think back to a few minutes before when I had just seen my mother try to walk down the corridor barely making it to see my dad in his coffin. The impression was so strong, and she was so heartbroken that she suddenly plunged and fell on the funeral floor landing flat on her head. She took a very hard hit and was hurt. Once again, my deepest fears ran through my like a bolt of lightning straight to my heart. All I could think about was losing both parents at the same time. The ambulance was called and all she did was tell me, *"Please do not let them sedate me or I will be gone like your father as well."* I was split in two. I had to finish my father's funeral ritual, but my heart just wanted to stay there with my mother. I had no other alternative than to send my beautiful mother off with my best friend who at the time was a patient advocate at the hospital so that he would stay with her and make sure that nothing bad happened to her. Meanwhile, without hearing any news regarding my mom's health, and only knowing she was taken to the ICU, I had to place my dad inside to get cremated. At this very moment all I could do was pray and believe that everything was going to be alright.

That was the worst moment of my life. I had to send away the only parent I had left, who was hurt and heartbroken, while I had to say goodbye to the one that had passed not knowing if in the end, I would lose them both. This was the moment in which I can say in all honesty, I have cried the most in my life.

The Lost Indian

I made a commitment to my dad that day, that I would make sure to take care of my mom the same way or better than he was able to, honoring his memory and to continue to celebrate our holidays and festivals with the traditional foods, treats and sweets, honor our gods and keep our Indian traditions alive which I confess my mom has done very faithfully and intentionally. Now during my mother's old age, I have adopted her responsibilities in keeping the tradition going and I make sure not to fail the promise that I made to my father and to myself. Life will surprise us with unexpected events, but during the strongest seasons we see the best and the worst of us shine. I did what I had to do to be an honorable son and I can proudly say: I fulfilled my assignment.

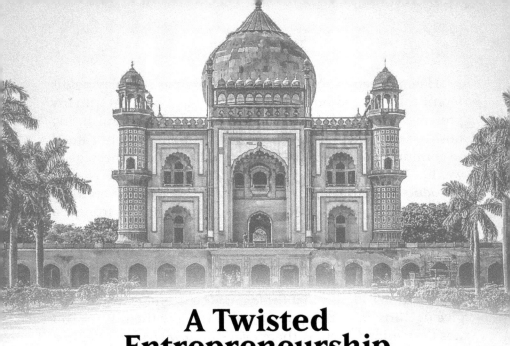

A Twisted
Entrepreneurship

Funny how life turns out. The introvert I used to be in my initial stages in life pushed me to now appreciate and embrace the extrovert I am today. The truth is I didn't always know what I wanted to do or who I wanted to be in the professional aspect. I only knew I did not want to go into the medical field. I confirmed this in school early on when we had to dissect a frog in the chemist lab! This was definitely not the calling for me.

Along the way I discovered I loved numbers and I had studied commerce and business administration in college, so I knew that something along this line of work was more suited for me. The college I initially attended was also very well known for their drama department and intercollege drama competitions. This was something that I would take advantage of later on in life in a more protagonistic role.

Having been exposed to the art of dramas and playing different roles turned out to be an advantage I brought into my professional career. It has been proven to be very helpful during business presentations in the sales department. I was not afraid to communicate, to speak in public, or to convey a message. It was like having a personal stage with a private audience. Now as a Product Marketing Manager I see the advantages of everything I learned along the way. Acting pays off when I am in front of a client and when I am running my business. I am able to take a product presentation and make it shine, while presenting the product that clients and companies have never seen before in a very creative and new way. I actually created skits for the sales presentations. I knew that these C level customers would only give us thirty minutes approximately to blow them away, so I was determined to show them everything we had to offer in a very different way. I knew that selling them our systems would be the easy part. So, we created three different acts, three different scenes or scenarios that we would act out in front of the customers. These acts would represent three real scenarios or situations that are common roadblocks for people that need our products or services and have not yet found the correct solution. These types of interactive presentations started to bring in sales and revenue to the point that I created my own presentation workshop for different sales groups within the company.

I found my passion within the corporate world. I have made a career of working in the information technology and services industry. I strengthened my banking skills, sales, customer relationship management, and sales management. I now have two managers that report directly to me, and I have a team of twenty-one people, in seven different time zones that I enjoy working with and seeing them reach their goals. We help different types of clients from a diverse line of banks and credit unions all the way from Hawaii to Barbados. To this day I still train many people with a two-day workshop, and it has helped many people advance their presentation skills. As a result, they have better financial turnouts for their departments and companies. Suddenly I had different companies hiring me to give this workshop to their sales employees. It was amazing to see how I was able to integrate the love and passion I had for acting and drama, with all that I had learned in India throughout my school years. Now all was integrated as a sales tool that was opening a path for me to continue reaching new milestones. For two years in a row, I received the Golden Cufflink Award as Best Presenter in my industry. They didn't give out this award on the third year because they did not find anyone else. I was the last person to receive this award so, to this day I can say I am the reigning queen. Recently, I've heard that they resumed with it in the following years.

Fast forward to my latest entrepreneur venture in which everything that I had learned in my college years in regard to people management, economics, marketing, and fashion, amongst so many other things; all of them put together were the tools acquired that now allowed me to be not only a business owner of an amazing establishment, but a good manager as well. I decided to take a leap of faith and open the doors of what would later become a safe place for many people.

A New Venture Is Born

When I first arrived in the Melbourne area in Florida, I started to look for a place where I could go out for a couple of drinks, spend time making good honest long lasting friendships, which I did find, as well as having the opportunity to be myself and have a good time. There were a few options, but twenty-five years later there were no LGBTQ+ bars left, and it was only found if we traveled for over seventy miles to enjoy events. So, instead of complaining that there wasn't a place, I created one!

I wanted to have a space without labels, an all-inclusive, judgment free zone. Little did I know was that even though I truly wanted to give the people from my community a safe place to be in and enjoy, today 80 percent of the people that come and stay at the bar are not from the LGBTQIA2S+ community. It is mostly always full of straight women who want a safe place to be in without being attacked or grabbed, as well as men that just genuinely want to have a fun time and even entire families that come to see the shows or play naughty bingo. Yes... I am the creator of the best naughty bingo in all of Melbourne, Florida. I had no previous knowledge of owning a bar beyond sitting on a stool drinking, but what I did have were connections. I had a team in mind, my marketing, business, and accounting background. All I needed now was how to make a margarita behind the bar!

Many good ideas begin on a napkin and in my case, they began by a pool over margaritas and martinis. I was sitting around with a group of friends, and we realized that we didn't really have a place to enjoy good shows, do some dancing, listen to good music, or talk with different people, while at the same time feeling safe to be ourselves in our hometown. It was there by the pool that I knew it was up to me to create the space. When I finally decided to look for a physical location, the first spot I saw is where today I currently have my bar. When I walked in, immediately I felt in my heart I had finally found the correct place to open its doors to people from all walks of life. This would be a safe place for men, women, and just anyone who can breathe. This would turn out to be a beautiful, no labels, all inclusive, judgment free zone. I didn't have the need to visit any other places because I had found my home. As I started to transform the graffiti walls and surroundings, I prayed that all who would at one point or another come in, would find a place they could also call their home. In simple words, my vision for this place was: integrating the community, having fun, and doing the right thing.

A Twisted Entrepreneurship

I started to play in my head with different names. I knew I wanted to establish not only a bar, but a brand as well that could later have multiple locations or become a franchise. The name had to be in a marketing forum structure that would be attractive to people as soon as they saw it, read it, or heard it in a marketing campaign. It would later be transformed into merchandise such as mugs, shirts, hats, hoodies, shopping bags, amongst so much more. I wanted this bar to also integrate food, so I invested in a food license and obviously a full liquor license. As I did some brainstorming, I asked myself what the most consumed meat in the United States was and chicken crossed my mind immediately. I knew I wouldn't name my bar *Chicken* for obvious reasons; that could be taken into many directions. I also didn't want a name that would drive towards a specific lifestyle. I knew that still today people enjoy themed bars or a sports bars, just to name a few, but I didn't want to fall into the typical "gay bar" stereotype or classification. So, I wanted the name to be fun and make people want to stop and come in. Suddenly the word *rooster* came to mind, and I thought it had a great ring to it, but something was still missing. I wanted the name to resemble my personality which I consider to be fun and naughty. I also love hosting events and bringing people together and some people would consider me a bit crazy in the best and fun way possible. Crazy chicken or crazy rooster just didn't seem right. Still with rooster in my heart, I started looking for alternatives and different synonyms. Then suddenly one day it came to me: Twisted Rooster! Done, sealed, let's go with it! I had a friend of mine who was a graphic designer, work on designing the actual rooster. I made a whole backstory for the character: he escaped a mental facility, so he is still in a strait jacket, he is ready to party so this is why he has on his sunglasses and capturing the all-inclusive message he proudly carries a rainbow mohawk.

I took all the necessary steps and legal precautions to make this a reality. My legal team made everything possible. Once I found the spot and now with the name in my heart, all I needed was to complete the process and my dream of following in my father's footsteps and becoming a business owner, would come true. I worked eighteen hours a day in order to make this dream come true. When I finally received the bar keys in my hands many people called me crazy, a lunatic and believed it would almost be impossible to achieve the opening I wanted, since I had announced I wanted to open the doors on December seventh of that year. I only had seventeen working days to make this possible. Somehow in the middle of the hustle and bustle of the holiday season, we made it work. The eighteen-hour shifts paid off. I worked my regular full-time job and after that, I would continue working on making Twisted Rooster possible. This meant working hard until 4:00am. Luckily, mom was still very healthy and mobile, so I was able to work full blast on the bar plans.

To my surprise, when the day came to open the doors to the bar, there was a full line of people waiting to come inside and experience the Twisted Rooster lifestyle. Finally, there was a place in our hometown where different people could come and enjoy without having to travel such a long distance. This included people in their mid- to high-twenties and up who were done with college, downtown, and bar hopping and were moving on to new phases in their lives and seeking a local place. They needed a space to have fun and I was happy to provide an option for that demographic so they could have a night life. I was blessed to have a healthy network of friends in my life that when it came time to start the journey, word of mouth was the main customer stream. Later, I created social media outlets to capture the interest of those that were not aware we existed. I wanted the vibe in the bar to be sexy, sensual yet horny; yes, you read correctly, horny! So, I divided the bar inside with different styles and textures. On one side I wanted it to be like the Red-Light District in Amsterdam, a full sexiness and erotic vibe. On the other side I wanted a softer, more beautiful vibe full of colors. I placed lights on the other side of the bar that change color every thirty seconds and glitter paint covers the walls from floor to ceiling. I didn't want to place any additional art on these walls except one special handmade piece: a memorial to the forty-nine people that were killed at the Pulse Gay Bar in Orlando, Florida. It is a heart with a forty-nine in the middle with angel wings, a rainbow, and my personal life slogan: *Love Us.* The hallways to the kitchen and bathroom are beautifully painted with murals that give life to the Twisted Rooster character. Everything that you see today in the bar was handpicked by me because I wanted greatness to be in the details from the glassware to the plates and bottles, everything! In addition, I wanted to have tv's with music and videos throughout the bar referencing the old MTV days. This would allow people to come, sit at the bar, watch the videos, and have a good time, even if they came in alone. I added along the walls different one liners of phrases that I use every day in my life, because it was important to me for this place to carry my essence. You are able to capture my personality and my heart in every corner, both inside and out. The surroundings of Twisted Rooster is created for people that wish to find an intimate space on the outside without missing everything that is offered on the inside. I made sure not only as a business owner, but as a person that needed a safe place to enjoy with friends, that my bar would become a destination spot for men, women, and families. The first weeks all I could do was cry to see this dream become a reality. We had a soft opening on the 6th of December and the 7th was the grand opening. It was a Christmas miracle. I made some mistakes along the way because of the lack of experience, like pricing correctly to have profits and what liquors to carry in the bar. In the beginning, you are still unaware of what your top demographic will be and what they will consume. You want to have a little bit of everything, including the amount of employees, to ensure you cover all areas and needs, which for me was critical because I wanted to make sure I covered all three main areas: bar area with all the necessary personnel to cover the kitchen as well, security and entertainment. This meant a good video DJ, event and show coordinators.

But as the bar grew, so did my knowledge. This taught me to never lose hope. It is a beautiful thing when it takes you to the right places and if you ever take a wrong turn in your life, find a way to make a left or a right but keep going! Your compass might someday breakdown on you, but that is when you learn to follow your instincts and values and your heart will never lie to you. Don't take anything for granted and always listen to your heart. I always knew that no matter how many roadblocks I would find along the way, it was never going to stop me; I just learned how to make a detour. Sometimes you will be surprised that the detour you will embark upon is going to be the most beautiful learning life experience for yourself. So, never, ever, ever, give up on your goals and your dreams. Turn your dreams into your goals, that will make the entire situation a reality. The hardest part will always be figuring out your dreams, the next step will just be working hard towards it. So, keep walking honey!

Beyond The Twisted Walls

I had always dreamed of being an actor and as you have already read, spotlights, stages, and audiences have always been present in my life. Till this day everyone says that if I had stayed behind in India, people know I would currently be in Indian cinema, no questions asked. This is why when I decided to integrate entertainment into Twisted Rooster, the drama outlet could not be kept out. I always dreamed about being transformed into different characters, different people with dynamic personalities, and adding the drag segment in the bar meant not only having an opportunity to continue enjoying and entertaining others through my transformations, but others like me would have a safe space to do it as well. So, from the furniture we integrated, to the props and clothing for the drag shows, everything has been bought with the intention of making people laugh, dance, and have fun. Whether you come in for the live singers, live music, the drag shows, talent contests or the naughty bingo nights, a swingers couples meeting place on occasions, just to name some, a safe place to enjoy a good night is always guaranteed. I have had the opportunities to dress up and perform different shows and I have given others an outlet as well for them to do the same. There is always something happening at the Twisted Rooster, and like I have said many times before, it is not just about me, but rather giving back to the community. I love seeing a family come in together and have a good time without the fear of what they will find. The atmosphere is always a happy environment and people can come in, have a drink, see a show, dance, enjoy a pizza or an empanada and have a blast. My two favorite nights of the week at the bar are Thursdays and Sundays. Thursdays because it is the night that I can find talents and see what is out there. Since people are always looking for gigs, it has turned out great. Sundays are more relaxed because of, "Sunday Fun Day," and we play naughty bingo. I get to spend the most time with the customers on this day and connect with them. We just sit around and laugh.

Laughter is very important to me and it's part of the ambience that I want people to have here. I have seen people come in completely broken and sad and they have come up to me to thank me for providing a great place and a good laugh because they had just lost their significant other and had not been able to get up and go out, and the Twisted Rooster has been the first place they decided to visit. On one occasion there was this lady that came in and she was sitting off quietly by herself on one of the couches outside. She seemed to be going through some issues. She could barely bend her knees and I spotted her. Me being me, I walked over to her and said, *"Darling, what is going on? Why are you here by yourself?"* She immediately responded, *"I am just very sad today."* I didn't want to impose but at the same time I felt like I had to find out what was going on. I was not about to leave her there alone to dwell in her sadness. If she had come to the bar, there had to be a bigger purpose. In speaking with her, I found out it was her birthday. I thought she was just there waiting for her friends to arrive and celebrate with her, but it turns out that she overheard a phone conversation where they were calling her all sorts of bad names that are not worth repeating and she had taken every bit of information to her heart. She was alone, heartbroken, and felt there wasn't a good reason to celebrate her life. I immediately took her to the bar with me and we did some shots. I told her, "Do not ever let anyone hold the pen to write your story. YOU ARE WHO YOU ARE! You have not come this far in life relying and trusting on people that don't belong in your life. Be you, be happy and let's celebrate. You are a gorgeous woman and nothing can stop you from living life to the fullest." The very next day she showed up at the bar in a limousine by herself in a Cinderella dress, kid you not. She walked in asking for the owner because she had not realized that the night before when we had been talking, I was the owner. She gave me a hug and told that me that she had taken my advice and she had booked a full day of self-pampering at a spa with all the works: manicure, pedicure, massages, she went shopping and paid for professional makeup and now she was there to thank me because my words had stopped her from taking her own life the night before.

There are many stories like hers, so many people that come in with one intention and have found within these four walls what they didn't even know they needed. It has been therapeutic for them as well as for me. Just a few words of encouragement changed her mindset to the point that she saw life was worth living. That she was already enough for the correct people and full of greatness and all she really needed was a reminder. I make sure that all staff members of Twisted Rooster treat our customers the best way possible. They have no idea what the internal, emotional, or spiritual needs of the people that walk through the doors are, so it is important for us to speak positivity, purpose, encouragement and above all else, love into their lives. You have no idea how powerful just gifting someone a few minutes of your time for them to vent and feel that someone has listened and can see them for who they are, as well as sharing some words of encouragement to them can do for their lives. I could write a full book just on the anecdotes we witness at the bar, but I can summarize by saying, the higher purpose of these walls are not the décor they carry but rather the people that serve within them.

THE PERFECT TWISTED PEOPLE

I have a dear friend whose life story has also been impacted by the walls of the Twisted Rooster. She and her husband have very conservative views, but they are very open minded socially. When they came across my establishment, they were blown away by how it brought people together that in an everyday setting it wouldn't be likely. They got to see up and close our "we accept all" guidelines and witnessed how people from all walks of life were able to join in and have fun under the same roof. Their sons come to bar all the time. Their oldest son, who served in the military and identifies as a straight man has said that he loves the bar because he is able to just relax and have fun. Their words to me were: "Jimit we admire how you have created a zone for us and our sons of love, acceptance, judgement free, and a special bond." People can come to the Twisted Rooster and be themselves whether they are straight, bi, gay, etc.... there are no labels. It's all just friendship and love.

With all of this said, in my eyes I don't have employees, I have partners. Every staff member that is hired is a decision between Scott and I because I believe there is wisdom in numbers, and I respect his knowledge and sense for people because of the experience he has. Scott used to live in DC and was in charge of opening a few Cheesecake Factory Bars, so he knows a thing or two about the onboarding process in regard to the job description roles we need. I on the other hand evaluate the tolerance levels they have for people of all walks of life and the human diversity. It's important to me to evaluate their essence and let them know that this is not a position to just generate a paycheck. People who are part of the staff at Twisted Rooster will have a direct impact on many lives. Part of the questions that I ask them is what their intentions with the community are because this is a very important an active role of the bar. Each member of the staff provides and brings something unique to the table and to the people they will serve. I always pay above minimum tipping wage, health insurance, paid vacations, even if they are part-time, including a plus one discount on all the drinks. I have also affiliated with a local insurance brand so that they can build their careers and have established a 401k, hospitalization, critical illness, and other health packages for them, so if they are going to be valued by us, they need to be of value in the community they serve.

Unexpected Surprises

Along the way something beautiful and unexpected happened. When I started to host the Thursday night amateur talent contest, my sole intention was to give back to the community a space and a platform that many could come in, share their talents (whichever it may be) from acoustic live singers, street dancers, drag and much more and they can be celebrated instead of judged. I decided to pay it forward to the community and I have been very surprised to see all of the talents that I have found along the years. They come, they perform, the audience selects the winner and there is even a cash prize every week. Not only are the people of the community involved, but like I said before, I have been able to create a talent bank just by giving upcoming artists a platform to share what they are passionate about. It has been so much so that I have brought them back under a formal contract for brunch shows or on Saturday night shows. My two main House Queens came from an amateur night, and they have stayed with me since.

This nontraditional space has even been the reason behind many people meeting each other and falling in love. Having the right people in place would be key and still is key for the success that I have lived as an entrepreneur. I have chosen people that have seen the best and the worst of me. For example, Scott, my right hand, has been in my life for fifteen years. He takes care of all the operational responsibilities because as founder and CEO I don't want to worry about having vodka or not, I want to focus on marketing, networking, booking events, and develop the strategies that will bring people in and help the business grow and stay open for many years to come. He has witnessed our beginnings when no one knew who we were, all the way up to our current success and to receiving the girls from famous drag shows.

During this journey and as the bar has grown, I have been able to create different strategies that have helped my business grow and reach the level of engagement that it has today. No one sat down with me to tell me or teach me what would work best at the Twisted Rooster. Like I mentioned before, I had never owned my own business, and had never experienced working at a bar. What I did have was determination and the best examples that came from my parents: if you can dream it and work hard towards it, you can achieve it. This progress that I have witnessed has been a combination of all the creativity in my heart and mind, the years of dreaming and visioning my own stage and personal theater and by simply listening to my customers, their needs and to the community. The best insight will come from the people that are at the bar, sitting on a stool and are willing to tell their stories and what they would love to see. There is a famous quote from Sam Walton, one of the biggest entrepreneurs in the history of America that says: *"The key to success is to get out into the store and listen to what the associates have to say."* In my case, my staff and customers have a strong voice within these walls. It's not only about what I enjoy doing which varies from drag to dancing and so much more, but of what they want to see and enjoy as well. That's how the Thursday night talent shows started, because of the people that approached me looking for a venue and a platform that would give them an opportunity. The naughty bingo idea for entertaining people from ages 21 and up on a common night, opening the bar for private events because people wanted to celebrate life and explore new options without the fear of having to hide behind society's standards and even to host weddings at the precise location where people have come to enjoy a drink and ended up meeting their life partners. Everything that I have lived from learning different languages and cultures in India, to having to overcome many obstacles and breaking through stereotypes and statistics as an immigrant in a new land, all the good and the bad have worked together in my favor. It all made me stronger and wiser. Everything makes sense because I have been able to use it all within the four walls of my business. This bar has been a school of life for me. I have bent over backwards laughing and I have enjoyed the magic of networking with the hundreds of people that have crossed through the doors at different moments in time. There have also been countless times that I have closed the doors of the bar and I just have sat there and wept. Each time I have done so, there is always someone there to help me pick up the pieces just as I had described before. Having those that celebrate you when you are little are the ones that deserve to be there to celebrate when you win big. Those that can laugh and cry, the ones that make themselves present and push you every day to be the better version of yourself that you can be, are the ones that you need to hang on to. Twisted Rooster has given me all of that. While I have the momentum to give this venture my all, I will. This is currently a focus of mine, besides taking care of my mom, and I will see it grow. I don't plan to be an employee for the rest of my life, but I do want to always be independent and a source for others to be blessed. This is my life project and when the time comes, and it continues to expand, I will see the best return on investments that started out by a pool with margaritas.

I see a future with Twisted Rooster as a franchise and seeing my legacy cross not only state lines, but countries as well. I can already see the Twisted Rooster in New York, one in California, another in Puerto Rico, the Caribbean, and Canada, as well as a food trucks to take the Twisted Rooster menu on wheels. The sky is the limit and if I had the opportunity to establish a spot there, I would do it too. This idea started amongst friends, and they have motivated me to continue this venture forward. This place has become a conversation place, a church for many, and therapeutic session where no one judges, but we all either cry together, laugh together and we always help everyone we can along the way. Summarized the best way possible: Twisted Rooster is a full experience that will make you become an open-minded person. This is why I have never wanted to have a label or a category that limits the experience. Many have said it is a gay bar, a video bar, a bingo bar, a dance bar, or a night bar... whatever it may be for each individual, that is what it will be. It will always be an all-inclusive spot. We do not limit it or categorize it because we believe we are not just one thing.

Another amazing and surprising treasure that we have witnessed firsthand is the joining of different people that have fallen in love, have become couples, and have even decided to get married after meeting at the bar. It has been such a blessing to see people fall in love and meet at the most unexpected place: the Twisted Rooster. We have celebrated multiple weddings and anniversaries of couples that began their story within the old graffiti walls that now carry a very special unity essence. and they are going on four years and adding. Many people have come back to tell me this was the place where they found love.

Their stories adorn the walls better than any picture can. Every time I have the opportunity to see people reach different milestones, especially those that involve such an important aspect of their lives as starting a home with another person, I am blessed to feel that I have contributed a small seed in their new life chapter. This is yet another reason that testifies that investing in a safe place for people from all walks of life was worth the cost.

Surviving Covid

COVID... the most feared word during the year 2020. I opened the bar in 2018 and in the year 2019 we were establishing a landmark in the community and business started really booming. I was barely starting to enjoy the fruits and results of opening the Twisted Rooster bar and seeing the first true revenues of my new business when all of a sudden, an infectious disease was reportedly coming from China and had already started to spread throughout the world including the United States. So many uncertainties, so many questions and so many feelings crossing my mind, fearing that my new venture was now in danger. What did this mean? What was going to happen now? Would we see ourselves like we saw the situation in China? I will admit that the noise seemed to get louder in my mind as I saw the daily news and heard all the updates and cases that continued to spread throughout the country.

You can start to imagine how I felt when the pandemic hit, and a total shutdown was ordered. I was not able to open the bar as usual and everything came to a halt. I couldn't stop thinking about all of the testimonies and what this place meant for many people, and now during such an uncertain time, we were all under a lock down and the safe place was now another closed establishment due to the worldwide pandemic. It was a mental challenge more than anything else because although we were not able to operate, the rents were still due, as well as all of the utilities, and I had the weight on my shoulders of all the employees that depended on the Twisted Rooster as their economic means. I had so many questions crossing my mind, but in my heart, I was sure that I had not invested so much into a business to now lose it. When I needed it most, my finance business side kicked in and I said to myself, "Wake up bitch and smell the champaign; I have to make this work. I did not work so hard to back up now." And so, I did! I started to think of different alternatives that could maintain my business and staff afloat. If I am 100 percent honest, Twisted Rooster would have never opened if I knew that my mother would be as ill as she is today or that a world pandemic was coming, but I know that everything happens for a reason.

I started to look for information and learn about all of the procedures, regulations, what we could and what we couldn't do as an establishment, and I brought in all of my staff to put together a game plan. Of course, I made a full power point presentation for them. I wanted them to receive firsthand all of the information they needed in the middle of this chaotic time. I made them the promise of doing everything in my power to keep the business afloat so that they wouldn't lose their jobs during this time. I didn't know what the outcome would be or if we were ever going to have the opportunity to reopen again, but in times where you sink or swim, I knew I would be giving my all to swim. I immediately came in contact with my CPA team, and they were amazing during these uncertain times. They moved quickly to request all available funds in order to maintain the business. The employees were also able to keep working. I made sure to source all available funds and resources that were available for them, and I even went out to meat markets and created baskets for each of them with three weeks' worth of meats, produce, fruits and other provisions for them and their families.

The Lost Indian

Something that truly helped me during the covid peak lockdown was the restaurant license that we had as part of the Twisted Rooster's diverse offerings. Because we also had this license and sold food, we were able to open up again once the order was approved, first at 25 percent capacity, later at 50 percent, and so on. Because we were not just "a bar," we had options to play with. So, I decided to get creative, and I got food trucks. I started to do seated dinner shows on Fridays and Saturdays. Even if I could only start with twenty-five tickets because of the capacity restrictions, I knew it was better than not being able to open at all. On Fridays, we had drag dinner shows, so I was able to give the drag community an income and revenue during the pandemic. On Saturdays, it would be a world foor tour with seated dinner shows. For these world tour shows we decided to take every Saturday, and we assigned different country themed shows. We did a marketing campaign. People could purchase the packaged deal tickets for all four shows, or they could buy individual tickets separately depending on the show they wanted to come see and attend.

I still remember that first Saturday that we hosted our first world tour seated dinner event. We had a full live band, Flamenco from Orlando, Florida, and they did a full Spanish flamenco show. The second Saturday was a Brazilian samba themed show and people started to spread the word and got very excited with what we were providing for them. These dinners just kept getting more creative and full of life and energy, something that was greatly needed to offset the sadness that the pandemic had brought upon us. A Moroccan belly dance themed dinner show was the third round that we did. All the food from each show was of course the representation of each country, so it was also a creative way for people to try out new dishes that they probably had never experienced and that they were tasting for the first time in the least probable place they ever imagined.

So, for the very last dinner show of the month I knew I had to do something big and extravagant. I decided to come out in drag for this show. I decided to create a Bollywood experience as the last dinner show of the world tour. I wanted to not only put on a good show, but I wanted to expose my culture, train and educate them about India. So, I brought in my video jockey and for two whole days we put together a whole production based on India. I made sure to share something from the north, south, east and the west of my country because there is something unique that you can experience at each of the cardinal points of the country. India is so diverse, and so much more than people can imagine. I wanted to make sure I put out a good representation of the country that I had the blessing of being born in. The entire show would be a drag show. When we put out the tickets, it was a complete sold-out show within the first eighteen hours of the announcement. I was humbled, excited and eager to show the community the beauty and the best of my country and I would be doing it through something that is very passionate to me: music, lights, dance, drama, and art. A lot of people wanted to come but unfortunately because we still had the capacity restrictions, we had to limit the people present at that first show. I did however repeat it two months later because people were still demanding and asking to see it. That blew my mind. This second show took thirty-six hours to sell out again.

We continued to be creative during the full pandemic season. On one occasion, I brought in piano players from Howl at the Moon to do a show. These shows were the ones that allowed the Twisted Rooster staff to continue to have an income when other bars were closed. People found distraction, laughter and even hope through these events. The media was so heavy with bad news, death, chaos, and so much noise that these events allowed people to embrace a time of peace, fun and joy. It was a safe haven inside of the chaos that was outside. We were the evidence that life had to go on. It might not be the same way we were accustomed to live, but we are resilient, and we learn how to change when circumstances change. We were not created for defeat but for victory. I made sure to continue opening the bar however I was able to, even through the holiday season during our first (pandemic) Christmas. I lost my dad during a holiday season like I mentioned before, and I know that not everyone views the holidays the same. There are people in mourning, people that are suffering or don't have anyone to celebrate with, so because I know what that pain feels like, I make sure to offer a venue for them to come, enjoy and have some company during the holidays. This includes some of my staff that enjoy coming in to work because of the same reason. So, we are here for all who need a place to recharge and have fun.

To this day I have not taken a paycheck from Twisted Rooster, I have always put it right back into the bar. During the covid peak season, I never had to defer any rent payments and I worked hand in hand with my landlord. I saw the divine intervention during this hard season over my life, my family, my friends, my business, and my staff. Just as the phrase says, where there is a will, there is a way. As long as I can be of blessing to others I will; otherwise, there is no point in having if you don't pay it forward.

ENDING

At the end of the road so far, looking back on everything that I have shared with you, I know that life will not always be easy. If you surround yourself with people that can make it a lot easier, you will achieve a lot more. Stay away from people that will weigh you down. You will not be able to fly high or fear less if you have people on your back weighing you down. The sooner you are able to identify these two groups of people, the closer you will be to soaring high and conquering your dreams. I always want to make sure to stay grounded so that I can be in the group of people that helps others. I want to help people find their love and feel fulfillment for life once again. This is the main reason behind my events, it's always about supporting the community and different charities. If I have been blessed and prospered, it isn't just for me to live comfortably, it's about paying it forward. I have done it here in the United States as well as back home in India because these are the two lands of my heart. My biggest takeaway from doing things like this has been helping a children's orphanage in India where the kids were all physically challenged and most were crippled. Others were mentally challenged, and all of these kids were placed there because their biological parents didn't want the responsibility of taking care of a crippled or mentally challenged child. They would leave them at the door of the orphanage as a rejected package for another person to receive. Having been a witness to humanbrutality made me more determined to help others in need. We sometimes think we can't change the world because of all the problems and challenges that exist, or the lack of resources that we think we need to do it; but we do have the ability of changing a person's world. When you are able to cause an impact in someone's world, that person will feel compelled to do the same for another person. So, changing someone's world will inspire that person to do the same for someone else. When we realize it, we are already changing the world one person at a time.

I was once asked what my biggest fear was and, in all honesty, I can say that it's losing who I am, and the only way that will happen is if the people I do things for bring me to a point that makes me stop doing it. That is my biggest fear because I do not want to lose being me and I don't want to turn into someone that does not appreciate everything that life is about. I don't fear losing all the wealth, power, or all materialistic things; but losing myself and my mom along the way does cause a lot of worry. I have had to work with these two areas because I learned that I can't be selfish in life with mom and the time that she has been assigned to be with me on earth and with the gifts and talents that were given to me before birth so that I could be of help to others in the world.

The Lost Indian

I am proud to say that today I have many roles: entrepreneur, business owner, caretaker, a busy social life, with many community projects as well as my professional role. I never imagined I would be able to do so many things simultaneously, but it turns out that what my parents saw all along was exactly this very moment. I always say, "Do it while you can!" So, if today I can run life with all of these roles and still have fun, why not? I do not pause. If I need a break, I take a vacation (especially cruises) or go to a spa, but as long as I can make a difference, I will. I believe that when you have the opportunity to travel to different destinations and experience different cultures, disciplines, mannerisms, relationships, networking, bonding; when you are given so much education with all of that around you and you don't put it to a good use, we should feel ashamed. I learned that if life gave me all of these opportunities, it is up to me to share it with others and with you today through this book.

Mom & Dad

Me & Mom

My Travels To India

Twisted Rooster

The best testimony is the one that comes directly from the people who have lived the Twisted Rooster experience.

"Always have a blast... fantastic drag shows and the owner is just fabulous." - EED

"Spectacular entertainment! Love coming here with my wife and friends! Truly entertaining!" – FE

"This place is so FUN!!! The bartenders are fantastic!! Security is on point and the dance floor is LIT!! Come have fun!!" – TI

"Not only does this bar have great employees and Drag Queens, but they are an accepting community where you can be yourself. Once I walk through the doors, I feel at home. I feel safe. And I finally feel welcomed. At every bar it just never felt like the people are full of life. At Twisted Rooster everyone is either having a good time or a naughty time. It's so fun and amazing!" – EJ

"Always a good time. Gay, straight, bisexuals, trans, lesbians, everybody comes together as one. I love Twisted Rooster." – JHC

"Fun place to be!... No judgements and safe haven. I can hang out alone and it's very comfortable... love Yah Jimit!" – CV

"Honestly my wife and I went there last Thursday. Not only is the crowd friendly and fun but the atmosphere is amazing. When we came in, the waitress asked us where we were from. The people we were with were from Brussels and Brazil. It was nice because they recognized our friends out of the blue and made them feel welcomed. The owner is an amazing man so friendly and kind. We can't wait to go back. This place reminds me of Pulse nightclub. All kinds are welcomed! We cannot wait to go back. If you live in Melbourne or in Brevard County, you must go try the Twisted Rooster. Brevard County has been needing a place like this." - SB

Editor's Note

Y ou might find it odd as a reader to find an editor's note in an author's book, and it is! But because this is not an ordinary story, I found it necessary to include it. When I started working with Jimit on this project, I was blown away by his personality, his heart and how easy people were drawn in towards him. I took it upon myself to interview some of the people closest to him. This included personal friends, people from his professional role and co-workers, staff from Twisted Rooster and even occasional customers that happened to be present at the bar. The reason I believed it was important was because at every single spot we visited as part of the writing process for this book, people would stop by the table we were sitting at, and they wanted to have a minute with Jimit. They all seemed eager and happy to see him, they would mention funny encounters and even stopped to ask for a selfie. It was through those unexpected encounters and the joy on people's faces that I knew it was important to let you know what this amazing human being has caused in the life of those that have access to him.

Speaking to his friends and customers was an experience I was not ready for. People sometimes forget to honor those that have caused a positive impact in their lives while they are still alive, and sometimes it's only when the person has parted that they publicly honor their memory. But this was not the case when working on Jimit's life story. These are some of the statements that they shared with me:

Personal Friend and Twisted Rooster Usual:

"I met Jimit through my husband, and I thank God every day for bringing him into our lives. It has been amazing to see how many people love him and accept him for who he is. I have gone with him to several company events and sometimes I just stand back in awe seeing how much people enjoy his company. Something that has always stood out for me is the fact that he is the same person everywhere he goes. He is able to maintain a professional atmosphere with his co-workers and at the same time bring to the table his charisma and his love for training and selling. When he is at an event everyone is always waiting to see what he has to say. He always does amazing presentations that keep everyone entertained, yet in the end brings in the results the company was expecting. This does not surprise me one bit because with Jimit, everything is always over the top. If he could put glitter on everything he would and that is what people around him love most. There is no way possible that your day does not get better when you are with Jimit.

I have never seen him angry, I have never seen him broken and the only times that I have seen him in silence, is when he is deep into his mind, wrapped around his thoughts. I love visiting his bar. Twisted Rooster is a place where I visit frequently with my husband, daughter, and on many occasions, I have taken my mother. As a family we admire his heart, his kindness and generosity and the safe place that he has provided for all of us.

The Sunday events are our favorite because it's always a positive vibe. So, because he has done so much, for so many people, I am waiting for the moment for the right person to come along and smother him with love because a person who loves so hard, deserves to be loved back in the same way."

Personal Friend and Twisted Rooster Staff Member

"There are givers and takers in life and Jimit is definitely a giver. That is his nature. And he is a true believer. He believes in people and when he puts an eye on someone, he goes off what he initially feels in his heart towards a person. If he feels the person comes with good intentions, he embraces them. Jimit is the type of person that goes above and beyond for everyone. It's just very inspiring to see how hardworking he is. I honestly don't know where he finds the time to do everything that he does, but somehow, he makes it work.

Those closest to him know that he always has three candles burning at the same time; all the time: his work, his business, and his mom. Not everyone that meets Jimit knows that he is a caretaker, and his mom is a priority. She is at an age that anyone else would place her in a home, but that thought has never crossed his mind. I know that he will have her by his side until her last breath. He always takes the hard road in life, and this is not the exception. I admire the fact that since he stepped foot in the United States, he became the sole provider for his family. He was twenty-five years old, and he was taking care of his parents, the finances and working towards his dreams at the same time, in a country where everything was new to him. There are many people I know that could never be able to do half of the things that Jimit has been able to achieve, not only as a caretaker, but as a businessman. I admire the fact that he has provided a safe place, no labels, no judgement zone for all people. He took the time to hire and train the staff to understand that we are the people responsible for everyone that walks in to feel happy and safe. There is no negativity allowed at the Twisted Rooster. We welcome everyone that comes through the doors, protect them, make sure to learn their life stories and value them for who they are. This also includes Jimit. When he is here, we make sure that he can relax and enjoy his time. When he is out of town, the staff makes sure to run the place better than when he is here because we are fully aware that we represent him.

Personal Friend and Twisted Rooster Usual:

"Jimit can achieve anything! I would love to see him grow even more and reach every goal that he may have. His eagerness to make a safe place for people to come together and enjoy is admirable and I can see the Twisted Rooster becoming a franchise. For now, we know that his mother is his whole world and priority. We see how she reacts after a trip and have heard how she brags to her friends about his bar and every milestone he has achieved. My husband and I talk about this all of the time, we do not know how he does it. He takes care of her while having two other full-time roles as well. He is truly a diamond, a very special person. We take care of him, and I can tell you he has a lot of guardians that watch over him. If and when a person comes that will be part of his life, we will all make sure that it is someone who can help Jimit continue to reach all the greatness that we know is destined for him. Jimit is not a common man. He has given us access to see how this community comes together and just shows us so much love."

Personal Friend and Twisted Rooster Usual:

"I have seen Jimit work hard and achieve the best results when he is under pressure. I have never met another person as spontaneous as him. I come here a lot and you never know how someone in the crowd is going to react or what things can suddenly happen, but in each case, Jimit seems to have four sets of eyes and two pairs of ears, because he always manages to capture everything and has the perfect solution. He has the ability to take the microphone and capture immediately the attention of a full bar without a glitch, no matter how chaotic it may be. He calms everyone, brings everything together exactly how it was supposed to, and it just flows."

Twisted Rooster Customer

"I love how I can come here and let my hair down without feeling judged. I have laughed and cried in this place, I have made new friends, eaten good food, gotten drunk, danced and have just been able to feel free and live life to the fullest. There is no other place like Twisted Rooster. I don't see myself enjoying a drink in any other place."

Personal Friend and Twisted Rooster Costumer

"Jimit has the biggest heart that I have ever seen. If he becomes aware of a need within the community, he will go out of his way to try to help. I saw him put together an event, a fundraiser for a fellow bartender that was trying to raise funds for a kidney transplant. He was able to raise over $3,500 for her in one night. His brain never shuts down and he is constantly involved in different charity events and community outreach just looking for ways to make everyone's life just a little bit better. He taught us the phrase "#loveus.""

Personal Friend and Twisted Rooster Usual:

"I have seen Jimit do so many things, his talent for the arts is crazy. Something that I have recently enjoyed are the Twisted Tales he has shared on social media. It's a blog style talk show to know about the juicy gossip that is seen, heard, and shared at Twisted Rooster. It is a crazy fun concept that only Jimit can come up with. He is the most creative person I know.

Personal Friend and Twisted Rooster Usual:

"Something that many people do not know is that Jimit is constantly helping people in the community and not just the gay community. He loves helping. He already sponsors drag queens that want to go into pageantry, sponsorships for education and many other things. He does many fundraisers to help others and gets everyone involved. He does a lot of community work."

Friend and co-worker:

"I have known Jimit for so long and I have always appreciated all of those things from his past that have molded him to be the person he is today. We have been really good friends since the year 2000 since we first met. We were both employees at a credit union. I had already heard about him because I quickly learned there was a trainer who made training fun and achieved people to engage with the material. And they did not lie! He made people enjoy the material and had an amazing delivery like I had never seen before. I have personally seen the benefits that he has gained from his acting classes and how this has been a highlight in his career. When it came time to accept a new opportunity in a different workplace, I accepted, but as soon as a vacancy came up for someone to do sales demos, I knew he would be the person for the job. He was immediately hired. No surprise to me. He became part of our sales strategies. The results that the team was able to achieve was in great part due to Jimit. We celebrated all of his milestones with the company. He was just such an amazing trainer. It was hard to compete with. People might not remember what he said, but they did remember how they felt when Jimit was presenting. I know that Jimit will succeed in everything that he puts his mind to. This is a man who started with very little and had humble beginnings, but once he arrived at the United States he never stopped growing and chasing his dreams."

Personal Friend:

"Jimit to me is genuine, compassionate, and real. We met through mutual friends and connected immediately. He is the most special person I know. He is always there as a friend with solid advice and lots of wisdom to share. He cares for everybody, it's his nature. He has the ability of captivating a room with a dominant presence. He acts like he owns the place everywhere he goes and walks in with a lot of confidence. As a caretaker and the way, he cares of his mom is such an amazing view. He has inspired many of the people the surround him with his love for her and just the details that he makes sure to have for her. He could have very well put her in a home because of all of the things that he does, but he decided to be her full caretaker.

I had the opportunity to visit the location for the Twisted Rooster Bar before he transformed it, and I can say it was a hole in the wall. It was nasty. The way he was able to see it in his mind first and later transform his vision into something tangible and beautiful was breathtaking. I was the first female to visit when he opened it up and it became my safe place. I could go there with my friends and drink, dance, eat, and just have a good time without the fear of being drugged or grubbed. It was a safe haven for all of us. Funny enough, I met my boyfriend at the

Twisted Rooster, and we have been together ever since. I always joke with him that I found someone before he did at his bar.

I have seen how this place has transformed the lives of many people. There have been many times that someone suicidal has walked in through the doors and Jimit somehow is able to speak purpose into them and change their life around. He interacts with them and gives them attention until they are able to see joy again in their lives. He has the ability of seeing the good in people first and the capacity to stand in their shoes. He has been through it all, so it's easy for him to connect with all human emotions. Precisely because he has had to struggle and work hard to get to where he is today, he never stops. He is always moving, planning, dreaming, working, and thinking about what is next. I love seeing his vulnerability whenever I can.

What I wish I could see more going forward is to see him taking some "Jimit time" and making himself happy besides making everyone else happy.

Twisted Rooster Staff Member and Mom Caretaker:

"Jimit is the best son ever. The number of details that he puts in for his mother's care is very impressive. He will always kiss her forehead every day and she will light up like a little child. He cooks all of her food everyday from scratch. He is a wonderful cook. He sits to watch her favorite shows and has lots of conversations. It's one of the sweetest things that I get to witness. I have been blessed to be close to this part of Jimit. He has set the bar high for all of those children that want to care for their parents."

This last testimony I left it to close this section on purpose. I had never been to a "no labels" bar, and I've met so many extraordinary people, but this particular interview melted my heart. I had the opportunity to speak with one of the House Queens that is constantly on staff making people laugh and enjoy the night. These were his words:

"Jimit as a person brings in a lot of opportunities for younger queens to come up and be known around here. He does a lot for the drag community. No one else has a home and nobody else knows where to perform. He opens up his bar and provides a safe place for all of us to display our talents and what we like to do.

Twisted Rooster has given me the opportunity to give back to the community to have a place to be me. I feel at home here. This is my home away from home. Here I have had many opportunities from meeting simple everyday extraordinary people to famous queens. I came out of a small town, picked on and bullied. I was the person that nobody wanted and I worked my way up to be the person that I am today. I fought against all that and did not take to heart all of the rejection. Here at Twisted Rooster, I am no longer the reject. When I hear people's applauses, and see how they want pictures and hugs, it validates me. They make me feel like a celebrity. It feels amazing. Jimit has allowed me to live the greatest feeling ever."

So, to finalize this unexpected editor's note, my biggest takeaway of Jimit's story is the impact that he causes on people of all walks of life. Many people dream about changing the world and find it almost impossible, but through Jimit's story I have found that he is already changing the world – one person at a time. This is not an ordinary story, it's an inspiration to chase your dreams, live to the fullest, be the best you can be, pay it forward and in the end, simply LOVE. #LOVEUS.

About the Author

J imit Kapadia was born and raised in Mumbai, India on April 9, 1972. Jimit assisted a British Catholic School which gave him the opportunity to learn the English language since he was a little boy. In 1992, at the age of twenty, he migrated to the United States of America with his parents seeking the American Dream. After seven years of residing in the United States, Jimit and his family became official US Citizens and has then developed a very successful career in the finance world since 1993. To this date, thirty years and counting, Jimit has shined in the FINTECH industry and today executes as a Product Solutions Manager. He is responsible for all sales, support, presentations, and services. In addition, Jimit is a professional non-musical theater actor which he was able to do through all his school and college years. Recently Jimit became an entrepreneur opening his first bar named Twisted Rooster, a non-label, safe haven for people of all walks of life in Melbourne, Florida. Currently there are plans of filming a movie which will debut as Twisted Divorce Party. Jimit has been full caretaker of both his parents since he was 21 years old and is still caring for his mother. This is the role he loves and enjoys the most. Now as a published author, Jimit Kapadia continues to add milestones to his life resume with the hopes of adding value to the lives of those who come in contact with him and this material. #loveus.